The Daylight Plays Tricks on Us

Julianne

The Daylight Plays Tricks on Us
Copyright © 2020 Julie Hoffmann (Julieanne Poetry)
All rights reserved, including the right to reproduce
this book or portions thereof.
ISBN: 978-1-7355089-0-0

www.julieannepoetry.com
@julieannepoetry

Cover Design by Julie Hoffmann
Interior illustrations by Julie Hoffmann

To my mother
whom I lost.
To my love
whom I found.
To the days and nights
that played with my thoughts
and to myself
for writing them down.

The Daylight Plays Tricks on Us

Julieanne

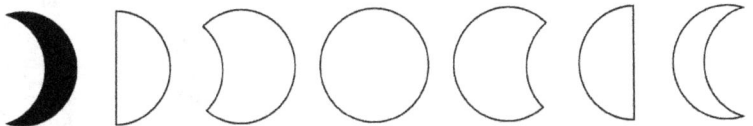

The Daylight Plays Tricks on Us

The daylight plays tricks on us
bathing us in the light
forcing us to forget the nightmares
we so desperately run from.
The sun warms our skin so hot
we almost forget the shivers down our spines.
The cold sweats between the sheets
that drench our minds in memories
we can't forget.
But the blue skies tuck them away
telling them sweet dreams
until the night falls.

Julieanne

My chest in flames
my mind blank
burning down.
Nighttime thoughts
that struck the match.

The Daylight Plays Tricks on Us

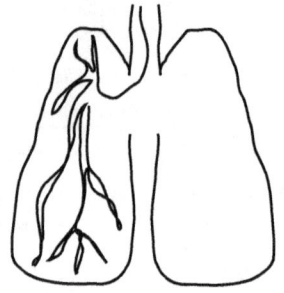

Does life keep moving
as it always has?
Do I keep taking breaths
after you've had your last?

Julieanne

The pain in my chest
it's back again.
An anxiety long forgotten
reminding me you're still gone.

The Daylight Plays Tricks on Us

Sometimes I just need you
to hold me and kiss me on the head.
A mother's touch to calm the racing heart.
It's been so long since I've felt that
I wish I took more time to enjoy the last.

Julieanne

The house is different
without your laughter - silent.
And suddenly,
I regret ever wishing
for an end to the noise.

The Daylight Plays Tricks on Us

Sometimes I think it's over
that time healed me.
But some nights you come back
to remind me of what I lost
replaying old memories.

Julieanne

Vinyl records scratching over
memories it hurts to feel
to music it hurts to hear.
Remixing moments I wished
could have played out differently
until the music is out of tune,
my heart strings pulled so tight
they just might snap.

The Daylight Plays Tricks on Us

Sometimes I wonder if you can see
the woman your little girl grew up to be.
If you can see the ways
losing you has changed me.
If you can feel the weight
of the tears on my pillow,
the heavy thoughts keeping me up at night.
I wonder if you could see me now
if you'd be happy with the sight.

Julieanne

Stop playing
and replaying
moments I can't bear to watch.
Moments when I became the monster
I always feared.

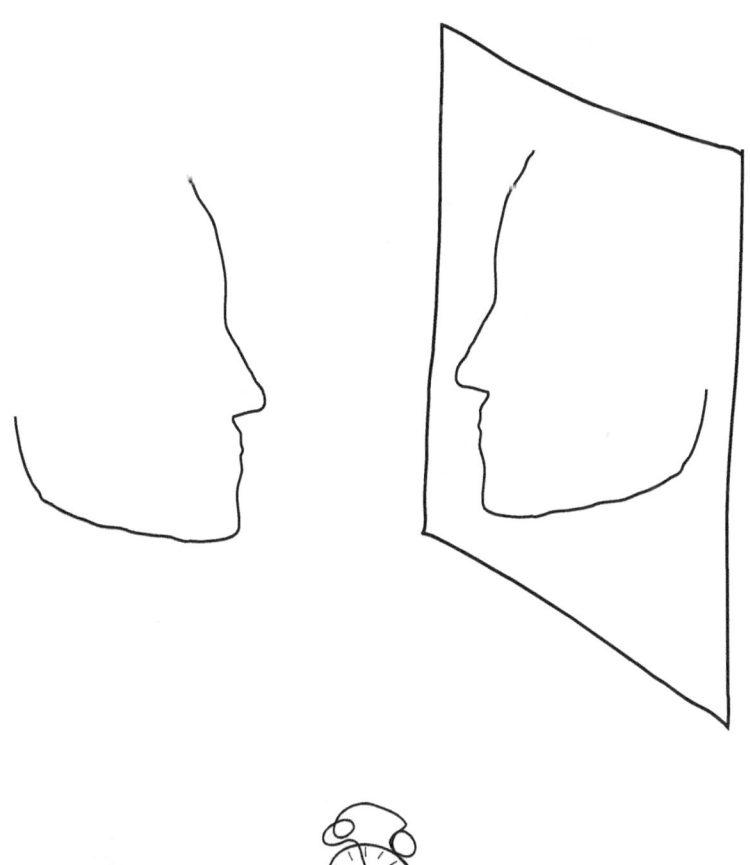

The Daylight Plays Tricks on Us

A trip down memory lane,
I pack lightly.

Julieanne

I listen to music to cover up the silence
of the words you would have spoken.

The Daylight Plays Tricks on Us

Julieanne

The Daylight Plays Tricks on Us

Daybreaks and my mind's suddenly a
blank slate.
The nightmares dripping from my memories
as I drink in the sun's rays.
New thoughts taking the dark ones' place
feeding me the hope of a new day.
Light soaking the ground where the
shadows once stayed.

Julieanne

Let's drink and tell stories of a time
we didn't know each other.
Stories of a separate life,
one without light.

The Daylight Plays Tricks on Us

Soak me in your memories
drown me in your soul
whisper thoughts you've had of me
hold my hand until we're old.
Be what I fear most,
a summer rain, no umbrella.
Pull me in until I'm close
drenched in you forever.

Julieanne

You make me a kid again.
Forging sandcastles in
sandboxes
I've long neglected.

The Daylight Plays Tricks on Us

Silent conversations make me think the most.
I read your eyes, you hear my touch,
we talk
I think.
I watch you hear the words I'd never say
as I listen back for yours.
In silence we speak
and I've never felt more heard.

Julieanne

Parisian nights
sipping coffee.
We muse about our dreams
and in the lights a lifetime passes.
I smile,
that's a life well lived.

The Daylight Plays Tricks on Us

It does not matter why you fell in love
it matters why you stayed in love.

Julieanne

It's that look I catch you with.
The one I wait for, search for,
and find when I forget to seek it out.
The one where you study me
learning every piece
looking for hints to what's on my mind
memorizing what's outside of it.
That look of love
the one that needs no explanation.
Just eyes meeting, exchanging feelings
words could never.

The Daylight Plays Tricks on Us

People write of souls on fire,
but our love is like kids on a playground.
A summer night
laughter in the air.
I don't burn with you
with you, I live.

Julieanne

Serenade my mind
like strings on a guitar.
A room of silence suddenly loud
with you in it.

The Daylight Plays Tricks on Us

Lyrics keep me sane.
Your words to a melody,
your heart keeping the beat.

Julieanne

I used to write of places-
ones that made me feel.
Rooms that stole my breath
views that gave it back
stories that soaked walls
filling them with life.
Memories of people I'd never know
stains of moments I'd never live
voices of thoughts I'd never think.
But no place has made me feel like you.
No room took my breath like your lips
no view gave me air like your smile
no stories, no memories, no voices filled me
with life like the ones we shared-
like the ones we made.
You're the only place that's ever felt like
home.
And so now,
I write of you.

The Daylight Plays Tricks on Us

Julieanne

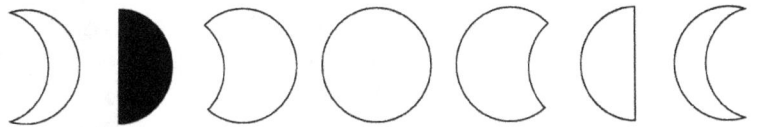

The Daylight Plays Tricks on Us

I keep checking for monsters
before I lay down to sleep.
So nervous I won't see it coming
when one comes to destroy me.
So unaware
that it has been me the whole time
hiding in plain sight
tearing myself down
night by night.

Julieanne

1 2 3

Awake at night frozen
trapped in my body
between sheets.
Pulse racing as I
count to three.
Slowing my breaths
every exhale taking
a part of me.
This sickness of the brain
the anxiety
toys with my mind
my body
as I wait for sleep.

The Daylight Plays Tricks on Us

Do you miss me too?
Wherever you are
does the memory of me burn your chest?
Because I am always up in flames.

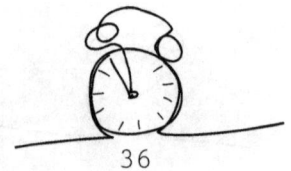

Julieanne

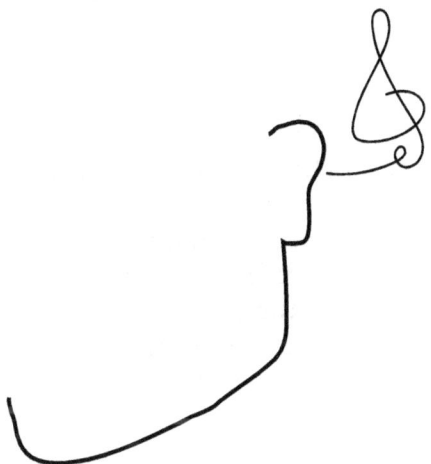

Your memory is a record I play often
drowning in the notes I'll never hear live again.

The Daylight Plays Tricks on Us

I beat myself up
with the same hands that
fed me strength.
Tearing down the
parts of me I built up.
Watching pieces of me
fall through fingers
that once held me
together.

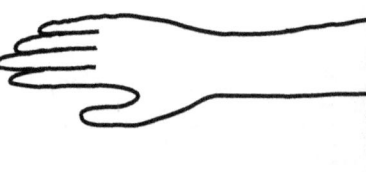
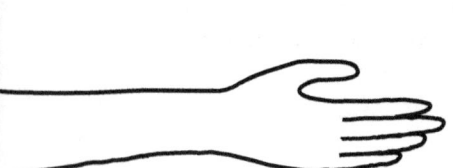

Julieanne

Most days you are gone
but some days you are here
and I don't know which I most fear.

The Daylight Plays Tricks on Us

I LOST YOU AND ME IN THE SAME DAY.

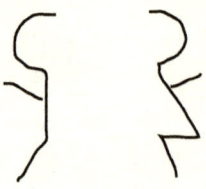

Julieanne

On the page is where you live eternally
within these words.
It is here that I come to see you.

The Daylight Plays Tricks on Us

I wonder in your absence who I've become.
If the young girl you knew
grew up to be everything you taught her to.

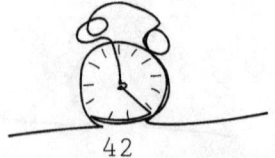

Julieanne

Waiting for the tears to come
left to wonder who I've become.

The Daylight Plays Tricks on Us

Fear has so much power.
I give into it more and more each day
piece by piece
until I am numb.
No longer scared of what will happen,
but that I won't even notice when it does.

Julieanne

Memories are all you left me with
to escape the numbness.

The Daylight Plays Tricks on Us

Julieanne

The Daylight Plays Tricks on Us

The alarm goes off at 9am,
my mind in twisted frames
of the night's dreams still
scattered on my pillow.
Daylight stealing from me
the anxious thoughts drilled
into my heart by moonlight.
The sweet warmth of sunrise
burning up alive the
tortured thoughts of night.

Julieanne

Take your time darling,
no need to rush forever.

The Daylight Plays Tricks on Us

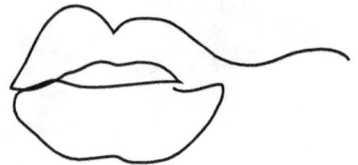

What's on your mind?
I'm hungry for thoughts
and yours are my favorite kind.
Feed me with the food I crave
with views and doubts
and the ways you behave.
Until I'm full spew words of those thoughts
a three-course meal
of ideas and arguments lost.
Dessert seeping with the sweetness
of a complicated mind.
Tempt me with delicious fruit -
forbidden is my favorite kind.

Julieanne

Your laughter fills the room
like wine in a glass-
always half full.
Its smooth taste
staining my lips
lingering as only fine wines could.

The Daylight Plays Tricks on Us

Our first date
I knew that you could make me laugh.
Our first "I love you"
I knew that you could make me feel.
Our first cry
I knew that you could make me stronger.
I don't need any more firsts
to know that I want you to be my lasts.

Julieanne

Nothing has made me smile faster
than hearing your voice
whispering my name
as if for the first time.

The Daylight Plays Tricks on Us

I like the way your head rests on my neck
the way you read me with no words.
Like a book with invisible ink
your eyes the only light that
turns a blank page to a story.

Julieanne

I used to think architecture
made a space powerful.
Columns that carried stone
arches that opened coliseums
cathedrals that housed stained glass stories.
Then I walked the city with you.
I realized it was never the stones,
it was the gladiators that walked over them
it was the centuries of fear and doubt that
filled those places of worship.
It was a feeling
a memory
a moment.
Paris was magic,
but not because of any tower
not because of any cobblestone street.
But because you walked it with me.

The Daylight Plays Tricks on Us

Coffee shop thoughts
music in my ear
you on my mind.
Sipping on the sweet
flavor of love
you left behind.

Julieanne

I fell in love
because of how I felt with you.
I stayed in love
because of who I became with you.

The Daylight Plays Tricks on Us

I never knew how much
I could miss
the warm touch
of your hand
on mine, us in love
feeling the heart beats
to prove it.

Julieanne

Forever sounds like just enough time to know you.

The Daylight Plays Tricks on Us

Julieanne

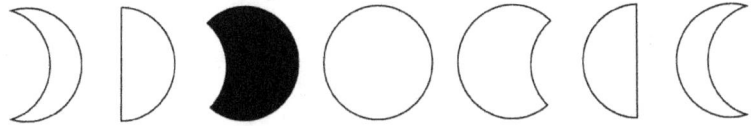

The Daylight Plays Tricks on Us

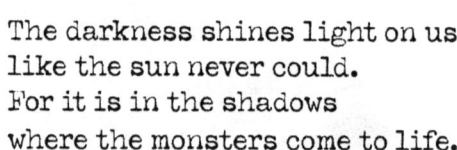

The darkness shines light on us
like the sun never could.
For it is in the shadows
where the monsters come to life.

Julieanne

I felt at home in my body
until a hurricane tore the roof off
leaving me to flood with water
filling my lungs to the brim
until I could no longer breathe.
The house caught fire
and suddenly I was up in flames.
The walls caving in
pushing me to my knees
entrapping me in the destruction.
The weight of the debris crushing
my soul as it was suddenly
homeless.

The Daylight Plays Tricks on Us

You painted lines
just to cross.
Built me wings
that turned to dust.

Julieanne

You chipped my glass at the corner
and thought no one could see.
But as the years of weather
crashed against my façade
the crack grew.
The rain began to flood
my insides until I could no longer breathe.
And you watched as my eyes turned
blue with water.
As my mind soaked through.
Nothing but damaged thoughts
left behind by you.

The Daylight Plays Tricks on Us

Words on a page
can't fade away as fast as you,
so I write.

Julieanne

I'M HUNGRY.
FEED ME THOSE LINES
THAT SATISFIED THE OTHERS.
GIVE ME THE BUFFET OF POISON
OF WORDS I'LL SWALLOW
AND CHOKE ON
AS I ASK YOU FOR ANOTHER.

The Daylight Plays Tricks on Us

Your lies like sweet liquor on my tongue
drinking to intoxication.
Knowing I'll wake up hungover,
but I give into temptation
every time.
Sipping on the words I know
are empty
waiting to feel full.

Julieanne

My body is made of glass
and yours of stone,
but you bring me to the dock
to weather the same storm.
My exterior a mirrored façade
your reflection bouncing back,
but you don't search for the seams
you don't notice the cracks.
You see what you want
you see what I lack -
the strength to handle lightening
and somehow stay intact.

The Daylight Plays Tricks on Us

Sipping on wine
knowing I'll awake with a headache,
but I can't stop drinking the sweet
taste of your touch.
The hand I used to hold,
now one I barely wave to.

Julieanne

That voice – liquid gold
feeding me words of doubt.
Darling didn't you know?
I was already full.

The Daylight Plays Tricks on Us

I lie awake at night staring at the ceiling
replaying every moment of our disagreement.
Analyzing every word
every tone.
Next to you but feeling so alone.
And suddenly the anger melts to fear
as I question if you'll still be here
by morning
or if the words exchanged have suddenly
changed
the feeling in your heart.
And as the fear grows
I forget why we even fought.
Left sinking further into
my all-consuming thoughts.

Julieanne

You can't be my sun in the morning.
I need to be my own light,
I can't risk being left in darkness again.

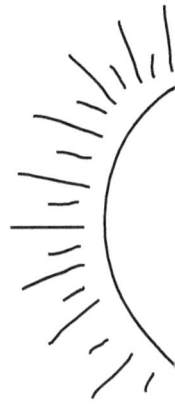

The Daylight Plays Tricks on Us

Julieanne

The Daylight Plays Tricks on Us

It's the morning seconds,
my face buried in the underside of my pillow
the sheets crinkled beneath my legs
the clouds drifting by out the window,
where I am most at peace.
Not moving, not worrying
just basking in the daylight
letting it wash over me
as I lay in stillness.

Julieanne

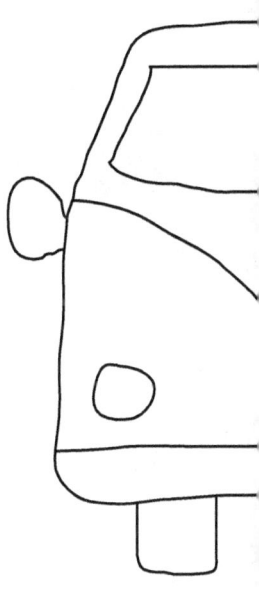

Four wheels and trunk full of dreams
was all she needed to leave everything.

The Daylight Plays Tricks on Us

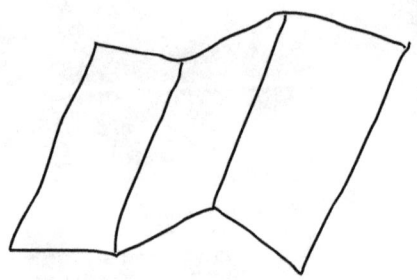

Gentle breezes
rolled down windows.
Just a map in hand
and no sense of direction.
That's where you find yourself.

Julieanne

Birds chirp singing
the tune of the
Sunday mood
as I lay in the grass.
Breeze flowing through the branches
sun soaking my skin until
it's hot to the touch
as I relish in your memory.
Moments that feel like a reverie
as they flow through my mind
reminding me of times
I can't forget.
Syncing to the tempo
of the bird's song
memories like lyrics that sing along.

The Daylight Plays Tricks on Us

And in love I fell
with all the small things -
with the birds chirping
with the morning stretches
with the hot coffee in my mug.
All the little things became the big
things
and in the tragedy
life was given beauty.

Julieanne

An unsettled curiosity will give you the greatest memories.

The Daylight Plays Tricks on Us

Adventure is born out of a desire
to feel alive.
With empty pockets and no plans
just a little love, luck, and hunger for
change.

Julieanne

My reflection is always clearer
      in baby blue water.
My eyes always more alive
seeing parts of the world
      for the first time.
Seeing parts of myself
      for the first time.

The Daylight Plays Tricks on Us

The trail I walked soon
came unmarked as I wandered
on uneven grounds.
The sounds growing louder each step
as the wet leaves crumpled under my feet
keeping the beat of the music in my head.
I continued with dread that the nightfall
was soon to call me to my home.
Afraid to be alone in the dark wood
I stood and stared into the distance
hoping persistence would lead me out.
And as I walked about I realized I felt safe
no more need to escape the beauty I had found,
I laid on the ground embracing the wet sticks
beneath my hips and I stayed and dreamed
until sunlight gleamed through trees
feeling the breeze, feeling free.

Julieanne

Journey the earth and its creations,
It's in those footsteps on unmarked trails
where you will find the way.

The Daylight Plays Tricks on Us

Play the music of the trees
shuffling in the breeze.
Let the melody of the
deer walking through the woods
be your morning playlist.
Hear the sounds you usually drown
behind headphones and conversations
and listen to the music of the world.

Julieanne

Coffee stained teeth and wine stained lips tell good stories.

The Daylight Plays Tricks on Us

Julieanne

The Daylight Plays Tricks on Us

Why does the darkness scare us?
Do we fear the monsters may come out
or that we may find it's been us all along?

Julieanne

WE PUT SO MUCH ENERGY INTO SEARCHING
FOR THE BAD GUY
BUT WE ARE TOO AFRAID TO CHECK
UNDER OUR OWN BEDS.
AFRAID WE WON'T FIND A PERSON,
BUT A MIRROR.

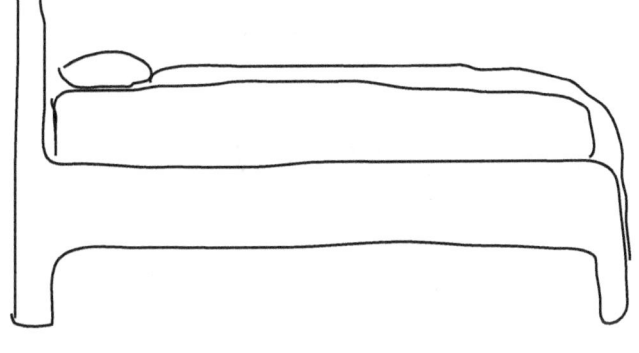

The Daylight Plays Tricks on Us

Sometimes I question my memory.
Waiting for your footsteps
to walk the house at night
hoping the day they left was just a reverie.

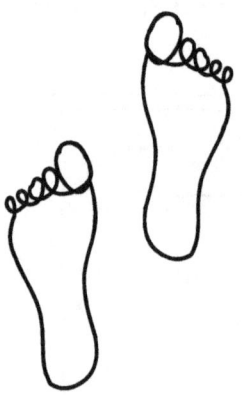

Julieanne

Music would flow over me
making me feel emotions I'd long forgotten
chords of sadness playing in my heart.

THEY SAY TIME HEALS ALL WOUNDS
THE CLOCK MUST BE BROKEN.

Julieanne

A sea of people and my eyes
go to the empty chair.
The one you were supposed to fill.

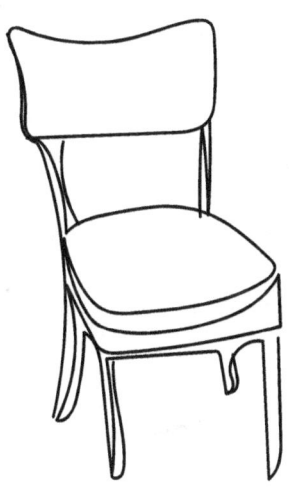

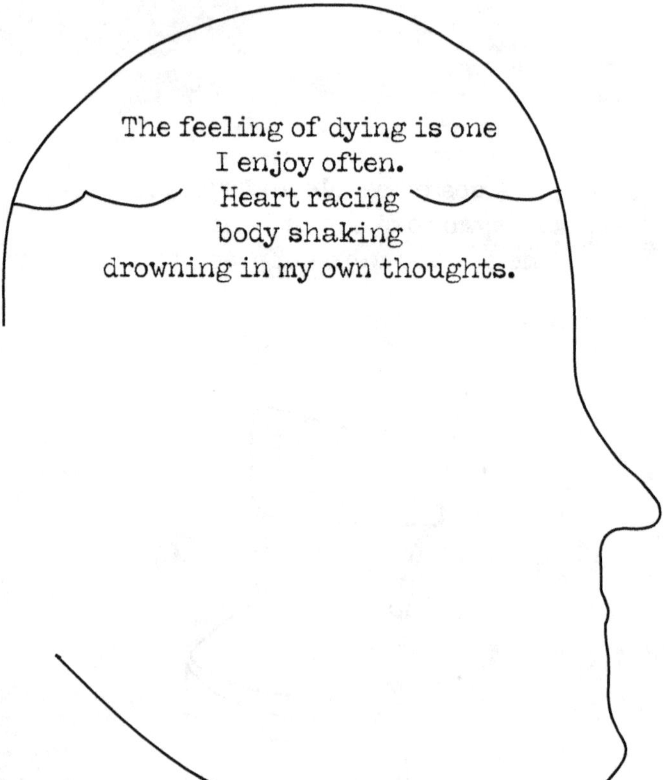

The feeling of dying is one
I enjoy often.
Heart racing
body shaking
drowning in my own thoughts.

Julieanne

Shallow breath
seeking for words of solace.
Anxiety's a sickness I can't cure.

The Daylight Plays Tricks on Us

I've been coming undone
day by day.
Parts of me I loved falling
to the ground,
my body carrying a mind that
no longer knows itself.
Circling around the inevitable
loss of recognition
as the girl I stare at in the mirror
looks nothing like me anymore.
Losing all ambition,
I seek to find the shattered pieces
of my soul
and glue them into place
as they were before.
But I question if the cracks will ever disappear
or if the scars of the moment I fell apart
will always be here.

Julieanne

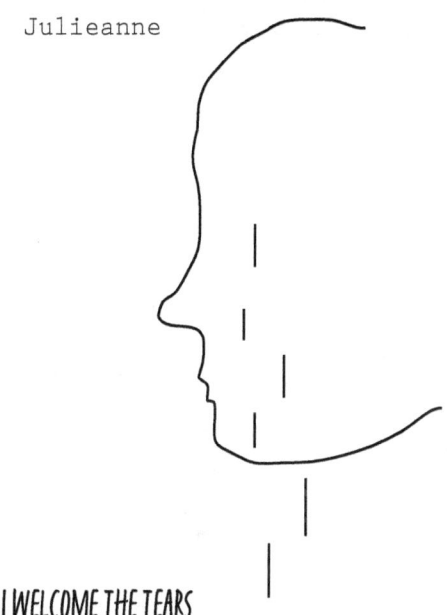

**I WELCOME THE TEARS
THEY'RE HOW I KNOW I'M FEELING.**

The Daylight Plays Tricks on Us

All these conversations with myself
asking how I feel,
but I never answer honestly.

Julieanne

Hard to admit but,
baby, I've been hurting.
My brain dissecting all
the things left unsaid
feeling like I'm a burden.
My sadness seeping into
your heart,
your beautiful golden heart.
So I quietly pretend it's gone,
that the pain doesn't keep me
up at night.
But I'm losing the fight with myself.
The walls carefully constructed
are crumbling down
under the weight of the pain
I've neglected.

The Daylight Plays Tricks on Us

Julieanne

The Daylight Plays Tricks on Us

The light shines brighter
after the darkest nights.
Just remember to open your eyes
when the morning comes.

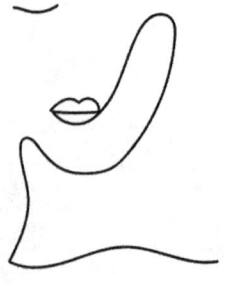

Julieanne

My only regret
is letting my inner voices
stop me from pursuing what matters.
The ones that told me I was not good enough
to make it.
The ones that told me I could never measure up
to others' definitions of success.
So afraid of what others would say
I silenced myself in the process.
So afraid of what others would think
I altered my own mindset.
So afraid of my failures
I crushed my own dreams for profit.

The Daylight Plays Tricks on Us

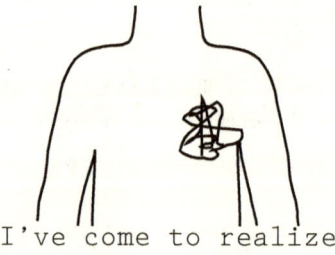

I've come to realize
the fear of failing
has never made me succeed.
It has only darkened the parts of me
that were meant to shine.

Julieanne

Tragedy does not breed strength.
It is your response to hardship
that makes you strong or weak.
Stop pretending that silence is powerful.
Speaking about the things that broke you
writing about the things that destroyed you
sharing the broken parts of you-
that is where courage lies.

The Daylight Plays Tricks on Us

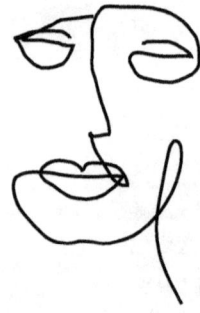

Stop searching the mirror for answers,
the girl looking back does not know you.
Search the passport stamps
the words in your diary
the miles on your van.
That is where you will find your reflection.
In the moments you've lived
not how you looked during them.

Julieanne

There is no word to fully encompass
the feeling of love.
There is no story that can tell
the way ordinary turns to magical.
No poem that can explain
the way you read me in silence.
No song that can replicate
the way my eyes light up when they see you.
So many words in the world strung together
trying to explain something
that doesn't make any sense.

Funny how words on a page
can change a feeling in your heart.

Julieanne

Look hard enough at the details
and the world will go out of focus,
but the cracks cannot tell you the full story.
They don't show the people kissing on the
corner.
They don't show the kids playing in the park.
They don't show the parade lining the streets.
The cracks can't show us
the life that floods the city.
We have to zoom out to focus on what matters.

The Daylight Plays Tricks on Us

Lose yourself to the lyrics
of a memory long forgotten.
The melody of moment,
its sound awakening a feeling
you thought you lost.

Julieanne

Tracing footsteps in the sand.
The wind erasing the paths
of those before me.
Left to wonder how long my
wandering will be bookmarked
in the ground.
How soon the wind will come
to take my story.

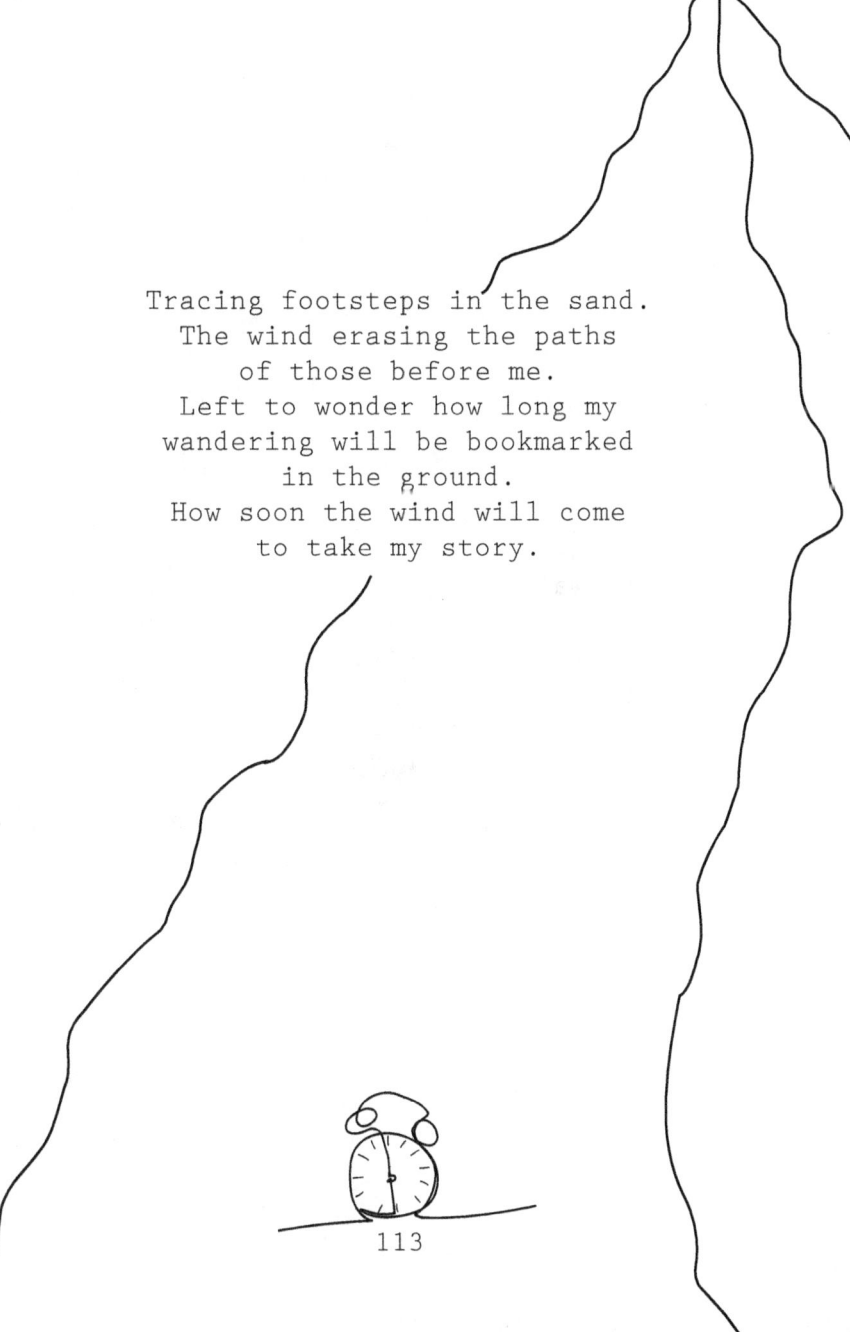

The Daylight Plays Tricks on Us

Find the thing that sets you on fire
in the best way possible.
Flames roaring to the beat of your heart
as it flutters with excitement
filled with ideas.
Find what brings you to life
what lights you up at night
and feed that part of you
until it ignites.

Julieanne

Fear only keeps your feet on the ground
your wings draped in dust.
But darling, you were built to soar.

The Daylight Plays Tricks on Us

Julieanne

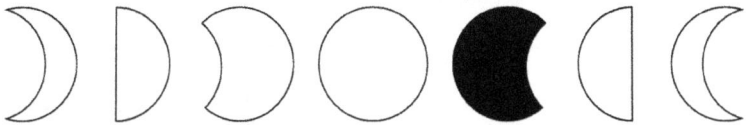

The Daylight Plays Tricks on Us

Sometimes the comfort of your own bed
is the scariest place.
It is there that I realize the source of the darkness
is myself.
It's tangled in the sheets
where I feel most trapped.
It's under heavy eyelids
where I feel most seen.
Maybe that's what scares me the most.
Seeing myself for who I really am
when the world is quiet,
when the sun is down.

Julieanne

My eyes play tricks
on my mind.
So focused on what's
in front of me
I can't see the
mountains I came for,
the ones I sought
to climb.

The Daylight Plays Tricks on Us

I am strong,
but sometimes I need you to hold
all the little pieces together
because I'm not doing a great job of it
right now.

Julieanne

I fear you will find all the parts of myself
I have carefully tucked away.
The broken girl I run from,
so afraid she will catch up to me.

The Daylight Plays Tricks on Us

Sometimes I lock the door so tight
afraid you'll walk through it,
closing it softly behind you
without even a last glance back
into my eyes.
My heart got so used to shut doors,
I bolted it and nailed it closed
refusing to let you go.
But trapped love cannot bloom
within the confines of a dark room.
And so my mind unlocked these walls
I carefully made
knowing I had to risk you leaving
in order for you to stay.

Julieanne

Whisper that you're proud of me.
Give me the approval I desperately seek,
the one who left me a lifetime to find.

The Daylight Plays Tricks on Us

Turn the lights out
and watch me spiral into
the shadows.
Pulling me deeper into
the parts of me I run from.
Tripping over memories
until I'm trapped in the one place
I couldn't bear to be,
the past.

Julieanne

To soft melodies
I come unraveled.
Notes with no stanza to fall on
my mind a jumbled mess of lyrics
I never sang to you.
Playing the sweet music
of what if's.

The Daylight Plays Tricks on Us

I spend too much time questioning myself,
feeding doubt.
Fueling fires of uncertainty
I never learned to put out.

Julieanne

Anxious thoughts fuel
my heart's
beats between the sheets.
My skin wet to the touch.
My mind nothing but numb.
As my body goes up in flames
to a feeling I can't tame
left waiting for morning to come.

The Daylight Plays Tricks on Us

Counting stars through my bedroom window
trying to calm the anxious mind
brewing a storm of thoughts to tear me down.
I wish to be the hint of light in a dark sky
that takes away your pain,
that guides you through the night
into the brightness of day.

Julieanne

I'm afraid to be my only source of light
I've had the power go out too many times.

The Daylight Plays Tricks on Us

Julieanne

The Daylight Plays Tricks on Us

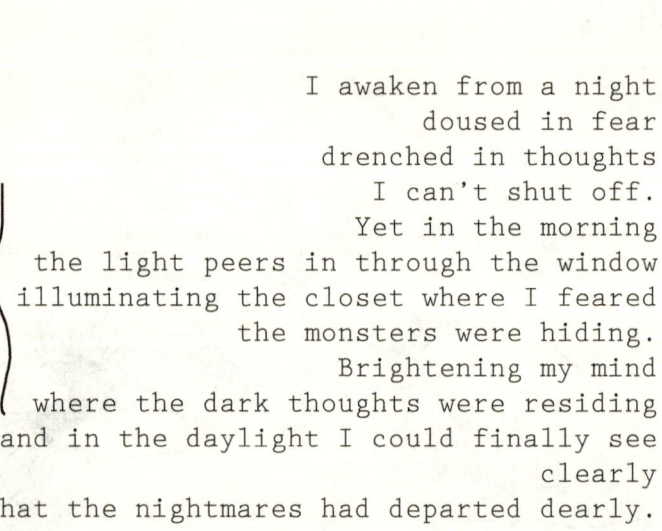

I awaken from a night
doused in fear
drenched in thoughts
I can't shut off.
Yet in the morning
the light peers in through the window
illuminating the closet where I feared
the monsters were hiding.
Brightening my mind
where the dark thoughts were residing
and in the daylight I could finally see
clearly
that the nightmares had departed dearly.

Julieanne

Stay the night
while I sit in silence
feeling her loss.
While I question myself
if I'm who she raised me to be.
While I wince at the memories flooding back.
Stay the night
to remind me
that there is beauty in love.
That the guilt and the anger and the grief
cannot erase the beauty.

The Daylight Plays Tricks on Us

*You make me smile
even in the pouring rain.
Knowing that only the rain
makes the flowers bloom.*

Julieanne

Words are the only way I knew
to explain how I was feeling,
but you read me without any
better than I could have written myself.

The Daylight Plays Tricks on Us

Thank you for loving all the parts of me
I could never learn to.

Julieanne

You didn't carry me,
you pushed me.
And in love I fell.

The Daylight Plays Tricks on Us

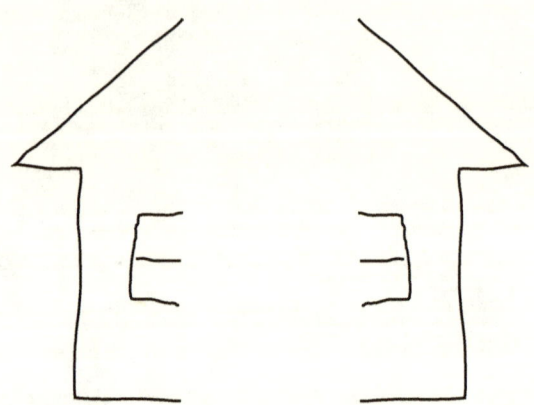

You turned a place of darkness
into one of light.
Took a home filled with memories
I couldn't bear to replay
and remodeled it in my mind.
Filled it with new moments
ones that made me feel whole
ones that finally felt like home.

Julieanne

Maybe the bad memories cannot be overwritten,
    but you gave me new ones to play.

The Daylight Plays Tricks on Us

Awaken the heart resigned to slumber
remind it how to beat.
Teach it rhythm and wonder
show it how to speak.
Encourage it to dream of skipping
disrupt it from its sleep.
Tell it it's ok to be missing
the part that made it weep.
Take from it the doubt and fear
of losing something dear.
For all that is lost does not disappear.

Julieanne

I spent years afraid to return.
Years afraid of finding the little girl
I left behind in the fire.
But you showed me
that old flames cannot burn forever
and the scars they left behind
made me beautiful.

The Daylight Plays Tricks on Us

The quiet moments
you lean your head on my chest
hearing my heart race
watching my tears fall down.
And you feel it with me,
so I don't have to alone.

Julieanne

Drift with me
like clouds in the sky.
No destination.
No form.
Just two clouds entangled
with the power
to make a storm.

The Daylight Plays Tricks on Us

Julieanne

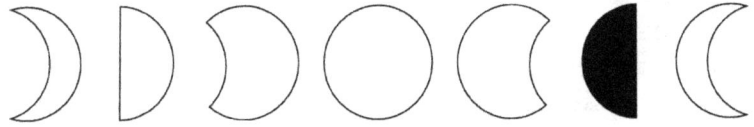

The Daylight Plays Tricks on Us

My heart beats echo in my pillow.
The anxious thoughts circle in my mind.
The clock ticks on as my eyes stay open
searching the room desperately for a sign.
Something to cool the sweaty palms
a memory to quell the voices yelling
in my head.
Telling me my darkest fears will actualize
as I wait patiently for heavy eyes
to transport me to the morning light
and leave those thoughts behind in midnight.

Julieanne

You were so vivid in my dreams
I almost forget it's been 10 years
since I've felt your embrace,
a place I felt whole.
Now I awake in pieces
beautifully unraveled once again.

The Daylight Plays Tricks on Us

Running in place
from an invisible enemy.
You stare into the mirror long enough
you forget who's looking back.
The safe feeling of home slips away,
the warmth of a hug
now a dangerous temperature.
The fresh air on your face suddenly stale
trying to imagine a future.
A day when you get to walk the streets
when things are suddenly clear.
But all you get is "somedays,"
hopes and positive thoughts
that try to hide the cage.
I fear when we reach that day
my wings will be gone,
that I won't remember how to fly.

Julieanne

Planted seeds and waited
impatiently
for roses to bloom.
Painfully
taking in the scent
of the moment I lost you.
I torture myself with reminders
of the nightmare I relive every night,
but it's how I know the dream before it
was real.

The Daylight Plays Tricks on Us

Asking for answers from a God
I don't believe in.
Waiting for miracles,
none of them to be found.

Julieanne

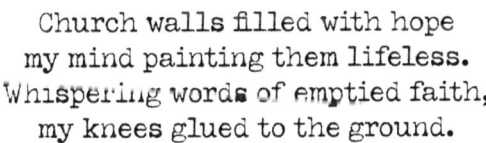

Church walls filled with hope
my mind painting them lifeless.
Whispering words of emptied faith,
my knees glued to the ground.

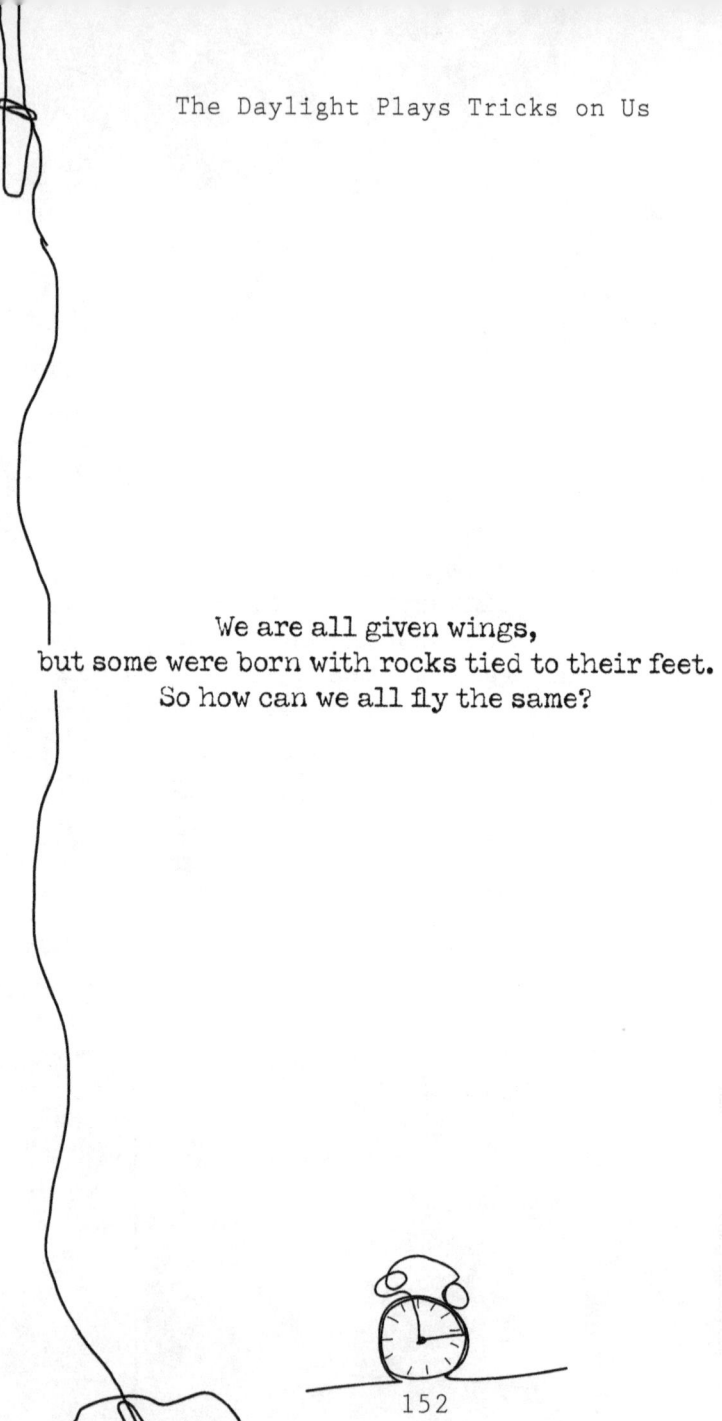

We are all given wings,
but some were born with rocks tied to their feet.
So how can we all fly the same?

Julieanne

Whispered words
and tattered phrases
run through my mind
on end.
Reminding me of lost
voices.
Once the soundtrack
to my life,
now only playing in the credits.

The Daylight Plays Tricks on Us

The fireflies take me to a dark place.
Roaming the yard with you
capturing their light in jars.
Nothing but the stars guiding
our footsteps.
Your voice playing the sweet
tune of motherhood
as I stumbled after them.
Bare feet tangled in the grass
forging memories I thought
would someday bring me joy,
now the light of the firefly
casting shadows I can't avoid.

Julieanne

So delicately woven into the
stories my brain creates
underneath heavy eyes.
My thoughts so alive drowning my
subconscious mind in
would be's
and what if's.
Awakening to a pillow soaked through
heavy tears carrying the weight of my
false hope.
Reality sinking in to remind me
the what if's
could never be.

The Daylight Plays Tricks on Us

In the dark it is hard to see
the ways in which I have grown.
The night pulls me back
into the place I've long run from.
A place of shallow breathing.
A heavy heart filled with loss
that burns so deeply I question
if I'll ever feel whole again.
But in the light I see that the flames
burning in my chest do not bury me in ash.
They light the fire that fuels my desire
to be better
to do better.
As the ash from a wildfire fuels growth in the forest,
so too did the fire in my chest breed new life
not simply destroy it.

Julieanne

Sometimes I hear your footsteps at night
wandering the home I lost you in.
I'm glad to hear you dancing again.

The Daylight Plays Tricks on Us

Julieanne

The Daylight Plays Tricks on Us

No matter how dark the night grows
the morning will always outshine
the shadowed parts of your mind,
the sunrise always bringing
your fears to set.
And as the moon and stars fade away
so too do the pangs of regret.
The promise of a new day
bringing your mind to rest.

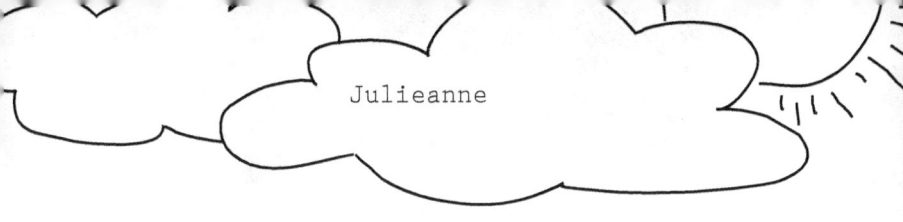

Julieanne

I always liked cloud watching.
The power to transform them
into anything my mind could think up.
The agency to decide what I get to look at
that day.
What animal I wanted to see.
What sign I was looking for.
To give form to the formless
to give me power
when I felt powerless.

The Daylight Plays Tricks on Us

All this time wasted
piecing together the perfect future
like a puzzle with one final picture.
I tirelessly searched for pieces
jamming them into places they
would not fit.
But life is not a perfect puzzle
it is a series of choices
mistakes
magic moments
that you can't force.
Time has taught me to stop
searching for the right pieces,
for the right image.
I have to make my own
one broken piece at a time.
And when the picture is complete
it will be all the more beautiful
because of its imperfections.

Julieanne

I found your diary
you write just like me.
Three decades between
and the words still tell
the same tale.
A piece of you I see myself in,
the greatest gift I could be given.

The Daylight Plays Tricks on Us

Years go by
separating me from that moment-
the one I lost you in.
And as pieces of your past
get uncovered from the basement
dusted off and looked at
as if for the first time,
I've come to find my fear
of letting you in
only kept me from knowing you.

Julieanne

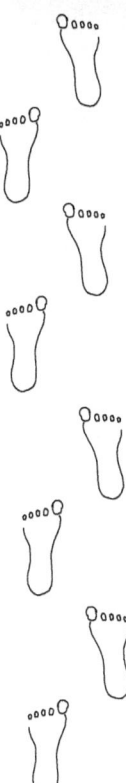

Moments that once filled me with sadness
reminders I ran from
now make me feel close to you in a way
I once feared.
For so long I was afraid to really know you
scared I would not turn out the way you
wanted.
But now it's in knowing you I find myself
realizing I grew up in your footsteps
even without you there to lead the way.

The Daylight Plays Tricks on Us

There are parts of me that
left the day you disappeared.
Pieces of innocence that
crumbled under the weight
of your loss.
Hints of happiness that fell
from my soul
and covered the floor
I walked on
so I would have to see what I
was missing every time I tried
to move forward.
Until one day I realized
they were not there to remind me
of what was gone.
They were there to show me the way
to placing them back where they belong.

Julieanne

I've always liked the feeling
of laying in the grass.
Sun hitting my face
melodies crashing over me
like waves
taking me through emotions.
Each note striking
a chord in my heart,
one that hasn't been played
in years.
And I lay there
until the tide goes down
and the sun sets.
My heart so full of music
turning moments to playlists.

The Daylight Plays Tricks on Us

Some days I hear you in a song
I feel you in the breeze
I smell you in the air.
Reminding me you're there
listening to the words I cannot speak,
forgiving me for the ones I have.

Julieanne

Waiting for the moment my heart
stops aching
carrying the weight of your loss.
A hole I can't patch up.
And as the aches get milder
as the hole feels smaller,
I realize that I don't want it to disappear.
Because even in the pain
life is better with you here.

The Daylight Plays Tricks on Us

The most difficult times are those
that foster growth.
These flames cannot be for nothing,
they are clearing the path ahead.

Julieanne

It is in daylight that
the night is put to rest.
Thoughts that kept you up
put to bed.
As you awaken to the sunrise
beaming down on hopeful eyes,
a new day lies ahead.

The Daylight Plays Tricks on Us

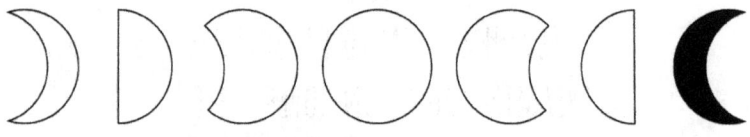

Julieanne

The Daylight Plays Tricks on Us

Julieanne

Sometimes words come easier on a page than out loud. Sometimes a blank sheet of paper listens better, judges less, and heals you more. I have found a safe place in writing. One to deal with grief, to express love, and to question everything. Like night and day, these thoughts ebb and flow, but the morning always comes. I hope reading my words can be as healing for you as writing them has been for me.

-julieanne

Other Books:

Proud of You

Follow my Journey:

@julieannepoetry
www.julieannepoetry.com

www.ingramcontent.com/pod-product-compliance
Lightning Source LLC
Chambersburg PA
CBHW031444040426
42444CB00007B/965